What I Know
[How to Do]

poems by

Michael Garrigan

Finishing Line Press
Georgetown, Kentucky

What I Know
[How to Do]

Copyright © 2019 by Michael Garrigan
ISBN 978-1-64662-046-3 First Edition
All rights reserved under International and Pan-American Copyright Conventions. No part of this book may be reproduced in any manner whatsoever without written permission from the publisher, except in the case of brief quotations embodied in critical articles and reviews.

ACKNOWLEDGMENTS

Publisher: Leah Maines
Editor: Christen Kincaid
Cover Art: Lamar Valley Erratics, oil on canvas, by Richard C. Harrington
Author Photo: Joey Ulrich
Cover Design: Elizabeth Maines McCleavy

Printed in the USA on acid-free paper.
Order online: www.finishinglinepress.com
              also available on amazon.com

Author inquiries and mail orders:
Finishing Line Press
P. O. Box 1626
Georgetown, Kentucky 40324
U. S. A.

Table of Contents

How to Create a Lake 1

How to Make a Mountain 2

How to Read 3

How to Read a Landscape 4

How to Survive a Blizzard at 8,000 Feet 5

How to Ask Her to Marry You 6

How to Make Breakfast for Your Wife of Seven Years 7

How to Go to Work Everyday 8

How to Sit on the Porch 9

How to Shoal 10

How to Sleep in a Tent in the Rain 11

How to Live Away from Home 12

How to Drive Down Gravel Roads 13

How to be Alone 14

How to Sit Around a Fire 15

How to Climb Katahdin 16

How to Wait it Out 17

How to Run the Rapids at Shocks Mill Bridge 18

How to be Married 19

How to Make Pizza Dough 20

How to Catch a Fish 21

How to Listen to Dylan 22

How to Listen to a River 23

How to Fall Asleep 24

How to Make a Mantra 25

> "We were standing
> Standing by peaceful waters
> Standing by peaceful waters
> Whoa Wah Oh Wha Oh
> Whoa Wah Oh Wha Oh"
>
> —John Prine

For Jess

How to Create a Lake

A breath of land
        an absence
                filled with water
A choke of rock and soil
underground veins seep up
        reach for emptiness
rain fills the rest, streams canter
to its edge. Put your hands
together and open your palms

How to Make a Mountain

Prayer hands push up and break the crust
and dirt and rock tumble across the back
of your hands, but keep the fingers together,
that is your power, that is where you reach
to and once your thumbs are out, flick them
to the side and there, now you have a ravine
and when it rains water will flow and salamanders
will crawl their way around the little pebbles of your knuckles
and there will be a river that rushes by your wrist that cleanses
that murmurs lines of dialogue and direction. Listen.

How to Read

This one is easy as I would have read
        to you every night probably *The Lorax* and *Road Trip*,
        the one that you flip over at the end and read back to front
        and the images that were one thing
        become another,
become another.
        This is how you read.
                Become another.
        If you're anything like your mother and I,
        you'd have found Kerouac or some anti-establishment equivalent
        during tenth or eleventh grade,
become another
        so in that regard maybe you'd have hated reading
        and loved the logic of decimals and zeros
something that your parents just don't understand.
        so this is how you read
become another.

How to Read a Landscape

This is important and does not require any effort.

Just notice
    and be aware of a few
        simple rules—
    Water is, eventually, at the lowest point
        and land will, eventually, bend to it
        and it'll usually, eventually, reach bigger water
        downstream.
    Watch the trees, even if you don't know their names
        look at the bark and where they usually stand
        and what they gather around, look!
    Thickets are thickets
        and a pain in the ass
        but they tend to border something beautiful
            isn't that how it usually is?
                you'll see.
Just notice. The land
    makes sense if you pay it attention
It isn't ours to write, but to read.

How to Survive a Blizzard at 8,000 Feet

Camp at the saddle between Lower and Upper
Devil Peaks. With first light, walk to the edge
of the lip where the Siskiyou Mountains lay
out like a tattered patchwork quilt, tips of Douglas fir
scratch the arch of your foot, the valley thick with clouds
cover Shasta's legs folded together, sitting straight.

There, off its right shoulder, that's the front that will bring
snow tonight. Last night, a meteor burning the sky in two,
tonight, thick snow laying heavy. Punch the rain
fly so your tent doesn't collapse.

In the morning string up a tarp over the rocks
that will hold the fire and pour your chainsaw
gasoline onto wet manzanita and weeping spruce limbs.

Light the fir pitch that you held between your teeth
and cheek as the meteor streaked, sucking its sweetness.
        Sweetness sometimes turns to fire.

Burn all the downed wood around camp
and drink hot tea—ginger, mint. As the blizzard
tapers and sun splinters clouds,
rub your cheek, notice the stubble of snow
that cracks each time you smile
in the sweet warmth held between
those rocks.

How to Ask Her to Marry You

Plant a garden
behind the house
in the old bed
that gets the most sun.
Till the soil, be careful
of broken glass shards,
wear gloves, or don't.
Wait until the broccoli
and onions sprout
and you're both
in the dirt.

How to Make Breakfast for Your Wife of Seven Years

Let her sleep in
        because she's a little bear in the mornings,
drink coffee, put on a record—Dirty Three is always a good choice
but don't put it on too loud—like I said—let her sleep in.
        Take the dog out, he'll go back to bed, then.
        If she sleeps past nine, start moving the cast iron
        get out the knives and onions and peppers and potatoes
she'll be down before you break the eggs.
        Pour half and half in the coffee measuring
        by its color, she likes it just a bit off dark,
        let it swirl and let her sip it and let her
        smell the vegetables frying and throw in some salt
        beat the eggs, cook the scramble, serve the dish.
Eat together.

How to Go to Work Everyday

Coffee and an easy commute.
Look for the sunrise in the long months
and the moon in the short ones.

Watch the river build with ice in February
and keep watch for those flickers
of headlights off deer eyes. They love to run.

Hot ginger tea, an apple, a line for a poem.

>   Pick the small things
>   easy to hold
>   and savor them.

How to Sit on the Porch

At night bats swoop over the shallow
horizon, little black smears on dark sky.
    Find the sway
    in their scribbles,
    look for patterns.

People pass by on the other side
of the hedges, the afternoon sun
is scarred by the forest between here
and there. Watch how light
filters through leaves, sieves of warmth
on your closed eyes.

How to Shoal

Arms draped out of window, fingertips tap to tires
gravel static crunch muffled under wool blanket
        the trees have buds
        the buds have air and sun
        the people have a dog reaching his head
        between them from the back seat
        the truck has a camper pulling behind it
        the ferns have dust from the road waving through them
        the radio has a John Prine song about Marie
        and blood in black and white
        playing and we yell Shadows!
        with him over and over Shadows!
        the river has water heading down to the Susquehanna.

        Here we are
shoaling in this moment
shoulder against shirt
neck against seatbelt
eyes against windshield
breath against breath,
        Here we are.

How to Sleep in a Tent in the Rain

A taut rain fly, a melody maker,
feel the gratitude for that thin nylon
that keeps you dry, let the taps
become an all-night song and when your back
hurts from the ground
and you wake up to roll over
find the melody and follow it until it becomes a dream.

In the morning, stretch outside your tent, settle into soft
wet ground knowing the trees played a part
—maybe the horn section—and boil
water for coffee, watch it riff, sip.

How to Live Away from Home

Take your truck or bicycle with knobby tires and find a dirt
road and follow it until you find a pull-out
along a river or maybe a lookout so you can see down the valley
and you'll notice that the trees are different, there isn't grass
and the understory isn't as thick as it is back in Pennsylvania
but rather, dry, and this may make you lick your lips and wonder
what people do without water and you'll think of home
and get a short little stab under the fourth rib that makes you feel
the slick diabase rock of the river when it's low in August but gaze
a bit further and know that this place is just like that place
it has a voice and an influence if you let it hold you for a little.

How to Drive Down Gravel Roads

It's all about the lean
and watching where gravel
touches grass.
The dust will cover
               for a second
the roadside ferns.
               Stay centered
as long as you can see what's around the next
bend then hug the lip of grass and gravel, a small kiss
      in the middle of nowhere.

How to be Alone

A bedroom plastered with magazine cutouts of favorite musicians,
at 5,269 feet at the top of Katahdin as a storm blows in,
on a leather seat pedaling up steep Pittsburgh inclines,
with her next to me in bed,
      behind my eyes.

The moments you realize you are alone
you'll remember your natural state
and this is okay. This is what you have.
This is who you are.

How to Sit Around a Fire

An altar, your altar
once you build it,
let no one take this from you.

It is ours, no, yours, a sacred spot
to stare into the burning of what is
and think about what may be—
        the noetics—
an entrance into the negative capability
the underside of what we see.

Remember those patterns I told you to look for, to trace?
That fire will reveal the inexplicable chaos of and beauty of
and shock of and deep breath of and hunger of and wholeness of
faith in mystery and in crickets that
jump from grass that grows from dirt
and wind that feeds the tinder
that licks the logs until they light the night.

How to Climb Katahdin

You have options—
Abol, Katahdin Stream,
Roaring Brook, Chimney Pond—
each leads to the same peak,
each takes its own turns.

It should be dark when you start.
Your pack should have what you need.
Do not get fooled by false peaks.
      That much is obvious.

Here's what's not,
      look for the pink flecks
      mottling the granite
      and the cleave marks
      that break the grain,
      the joining of mineral and color.

The ground holds your balance,
the mountain pushes your heels
into the next step up into scraggly
fir and bilberry, trees turn to tundra,
the clouds are there, at your lips.

How to Wait it Out

Did you notice
        the full worm moon
linger all night
        stalking the day
before?

Be careful of those nights
        that help you forget
that we walk on the dirt of ancestors
        and speak syllables of oak bones, ghosts.

How to Run the Rapids at Shocks Mill Bridge

In low water paddle river right, count
three trestles from the bank, aim
for the middle, boulders will frame
each pillar. Ride the confluence of Codorus
Creek and the Susquehanna. Follow foam lines.

In high water stay river left,
skirt between Pole Island and the corn
fields cradling purple loosestrife and hibiscus,
count three trestles from the left, the last
one before the rock outcropping that blocks
the fourth and fifth.

Follow foam lines, those mergings of marbled
water, where tributaries meet their end,
where currents collide. Let yourself
ride on the palm of the river.

How to be Married

Think of it as dry stone masonry
where you build steps up trails
and walls that hold the ground
with boulders and pebbles—
weight on weight
> a nestle in a crook
> a stable slab
> small rock to backfill
> and mix with dirt
> something that
> holds the erosion
> that gets stronger
> with each flood.

How to Make Pizza Dough

Measuring
is rarely important.
        things line up
        the way they do.

Get local honey, quick yeast, dry mozzarella,
your favorite toppings, sauce (not too runny).
Pull the mixing bowl your mother gave you
from the cupboard, pour in warm tap water until
the ceiling fan reflects in it. Spell out your word
with the honey, tilt in a spoonful of yeast.

Let it sit until it gets murky. Remember that murkiness
is just the debris of experience, of the friction of a moment.
Let it settle until you flip the record
        caught in the dead wax of Side A.

Pinch salt, add olive oil, start
cupping in flour and mixing
        flaky, too dry.
        sticky, too wet.

Kneed it for a good while,
let it rise for a couple of hours.
Let the settling become a beginning.

How to Catch a Fish

Go to the water with a rod,
        no matter if it's a fly rod or a spinning rod,
Just have something on the end of the line—
        a lure, a fly—
Stand by the water. Watch it a bit,
get a feel for how it moves over the rock.
See, there are little bugs flitting through the air behind that one
in the slow water, a pocket, you know,
where we keep stuff like our keys,
the river keeps its bugs and its fish, slow enough to rest,
try to get your line into it, let it sink, nudge it, play it a bit
you'll get the hang of it, just make it look like it's supposed to be there,
        keep casting and retrieving
and when you feel a pause or a strike, set the hook, move the rod up
or to the side but not too hard, let the fish tell you what it needs to do,
dance with it a bit, you won't own it, you'll coax it
closer and closer until you can gently hold it in the water
and remove the hook and trace the patterns the water has carved
across its skin.

        We have these patterns as well,
            most are on the inside and some of us try to trace them,
                find yours, trace them.
        Look for those slow soft spots.
        That is where you find goodness.

How to Listen to Dylan

You should start with one of his 60's albums, probably *Highway 61 Revisited* because that was the first one I bought off a recommendation of a stoner record store owner who knew how to turn a kid with cash from mowing grass onto good music and he ended up influencing my life more than any teacher, really—don't lose sight of how one little moment that may seem insignificant at the time can end up moving the arc of your story—and be sure to listen closely to "Queen Jane" and "It Takes a Lot to Laugh" as these songs are the basis of his later years and they'll turn you on to other great artists like Garcia and Sun Ra and Gillian Welch and memorize at least two stanzas from "Desolation Row" so you have something to sing back to yourself waiting in lines trying not to stare at your phone. Once you have that record down and your heart has been broken or is about to be or maybe you just want to know what love might be like then you'll want to listen to *Blood on the Tracks* and, yeah, "Tangled Up in Blue" is great and you'll want to know all those words and all the various iterations of them but don't sleep on "Shelter from the Storm" because, damnit, it's fucking beautiful and it kills me every time and the chords are so goddamned simple just like love really should be. Just listen. If you're anything like me you'll latch onto *Time Out of Mind* and its murk because life is like that most times, just kind of gray and filled with sediment and those times when that murkiness settles and the water clears, well that's "Highlands" and maybe you'll listen to it as a teenager and like the riff and maybe you'll drink a glass of whiskey in your twenties and like the hard-boiled egg stanza and each year adds a layer to that song. Eventually you'll realize that the 80's had some gems and even '79 had *Street Legal* which is a masterpiece of desire and existential crisis and then you'll listened to "Senor" and you'll be there, in that half lit vacant lot near the border and eventually you'll hone in on a few albums and they're always there. Songs for everything.

How to Listen to a River

The complexity of a riffle
        the puzzle of granite boulders
the downed poplar
        the swallow on the branch overhanging
                the bank.

What you see is a clue as to what you'll hear.
But close your eyes at some point, hopefully
with water running over your ankles
and feel the weight of the downstream pull
and how you sink into the pebbled stream bed.

It is an all-encompassing sound, this river.

How to Fall Asleep

With the trains that track their way along the river
        sink into that lullaby rustle
                steel and iron
                rust and blues.

The three hoots of a horned owl
        call in dreams
               it is these that you need.

How to Make a Mantra

Everything worth knowing
has one, locusts need the heat
of summer, frogs need the cool wet
slough of spring, oaks need the long sun.

What you have is what you need,
a before, a between, an after—repeat—
repeat the song of the river running
from the lake of your palms and the ravines
of your mountains stretching across the landscape
of your life until you find your cadence.
      Sink into your steps.

Michael **Garrigan** writes and teaches along the banks of the Susquehanna River in Pennsylvania. He spends most of his free time exploring the river's many tributaries with a fly rod. When he's not on the water or in front of students, he can usually be found hiking the riverlands and exploring the Pennsylvania wilds with his wife, Jess, and dog, Whitman. He once spent three years working trails in Maine, Colorado, and California where he learned to use a pen and Pulaski. Each summer he goes to dirt and camps around the country in search of wild water and good burritos. He enjoys watching water move over rocks and feels strongly that every watershed should have a Poet Laureate.

Michael holds a BA in Creative Writing from the University of Pittsburgh and an MA in English & Creative Writing from Southern New Hampshire University. His essays and poetry have appeared in publications such as *Gray's Sporting Journal, The Wayfarer, The Drake Magazine, Hawk & Handsaw Journal of Creative Sustainability, Sky Island Journal, Barren Magazine, Split Rock Review,* and other magazines and anthologies. You can find more of his writing at www.mgarrigan.com.

www.ingramcontent.com/pod-product-compliance
Lightning Source LLC
LaVergne TN
LVHW041518070426
835507LV00012B/1660